By: Jobe Leonard

For information about special discounts, bulk purchases, or autographed editions please contact Jobe Leonard at

Jobe@LakeFun.com

Write to:

Lake Fun

1511 Mayflower Lane

Dandridge, TN 37725

Or visit:

www.LakeFun.com

Binoculars

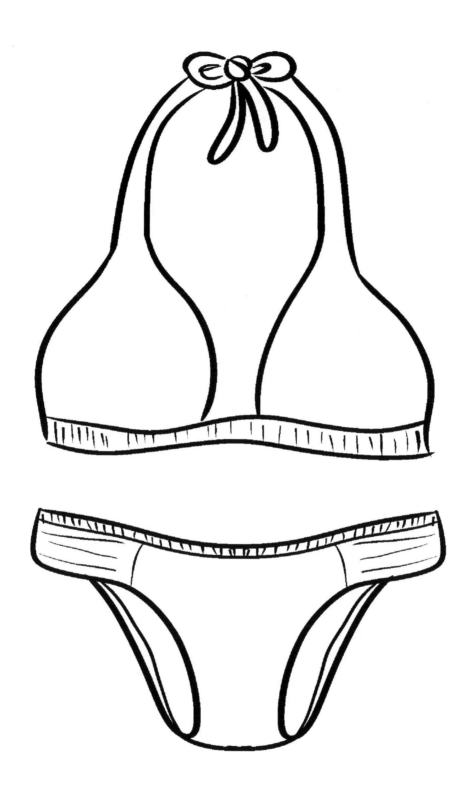

Bikini

Anchor

Bag of Ice

Lake Towel

Bug Spray

Book

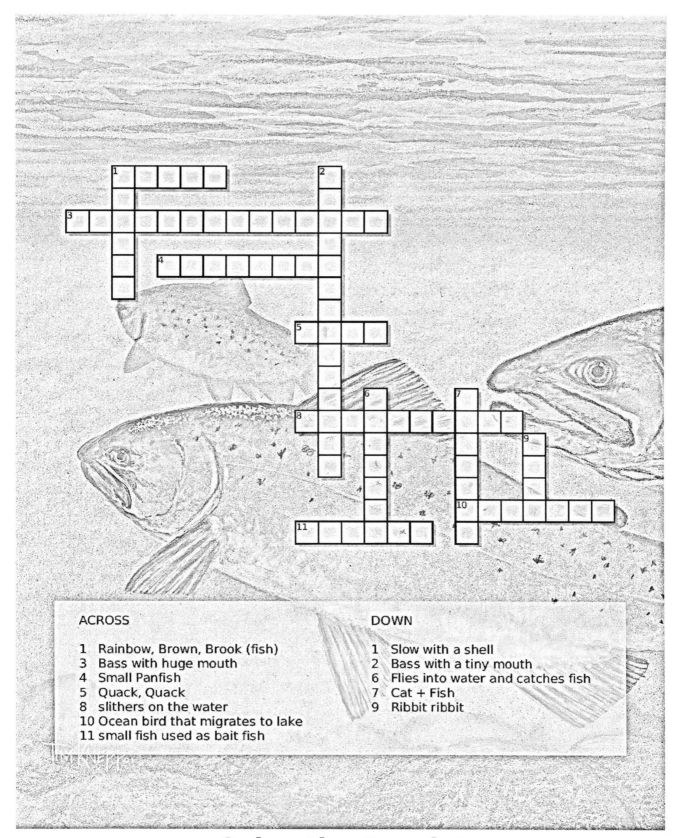

ACROSS

1 Rainbow, Brown, Brook (fish)
3 Bass with huge mouth
4 Small Panfish
5 Quack, Quack
8 slithers on the water
10 Ocean bird that migrates to lake
11 small fish used as bait fish

DOWN

1 Slow with a shell
2 Bass with a tiny mouth
6 Flies into water and catches fish
7 Cat + Fish
9 Ribbit ribbit

Solve the Puzzle!

Bobber

Row Boat

Drinks

Dog

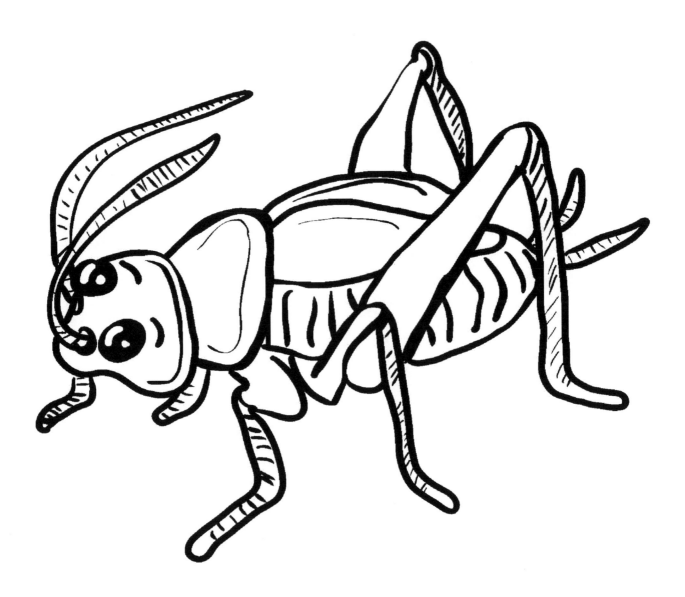

Cricket

J	D	V	A	F	R	I	E	N	D	S	P	U	C
F	G	F	U	I	C	A	M	P		F	I	R	E
M	I	O	C	S	W	W	M	O	N	E	Y	J	E
Z	N	S	G	H	S	Y	A	L	T	D	J	M	I
F	I	D	H	G	W	W	T	O	U	X	T	R	V
P	G	D	R	E	L	V	M	T	B	O	R	T	J
A	R	D	R	I	R	E	O	I	E	P	U	E	W
D	I	V	A	B	N	M	S	O	S	I	N	N	H
D	L	I	D	O	B	K	A	N	V	S	K	T	A
L	L	S	I	A	P	P	S	N	E	J	S	A	T
E	W	O	O	T	P	Q	D	B	I	K	I	N	I
F	I	R	E		W	O	O	D	J	Z	Q	M	V
G	X	F	L	F	L	I	P	P	E	R	S	W	V
H	S	B	T	O	W	E	L	R	A	F	T	S	X

How Many Lake Fun Words Can You Find?

Coozie

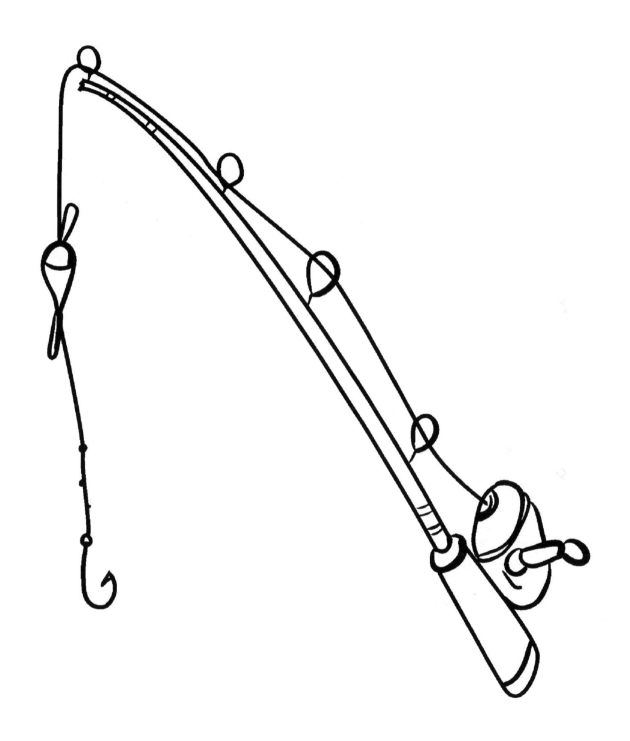

Fishing Rod

Fishing Hook

Fishing Boat

Fisherman

Circle Your Favorite Lake Fun Activities!

Hat

Grill

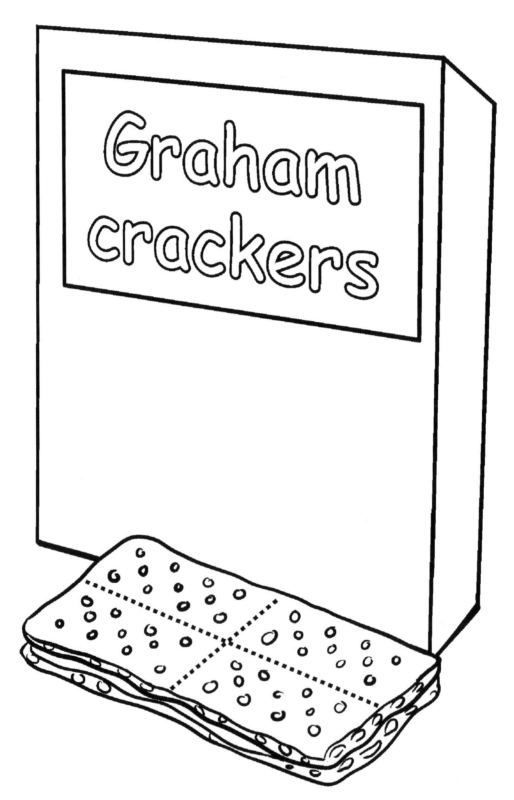

Graham Crackers

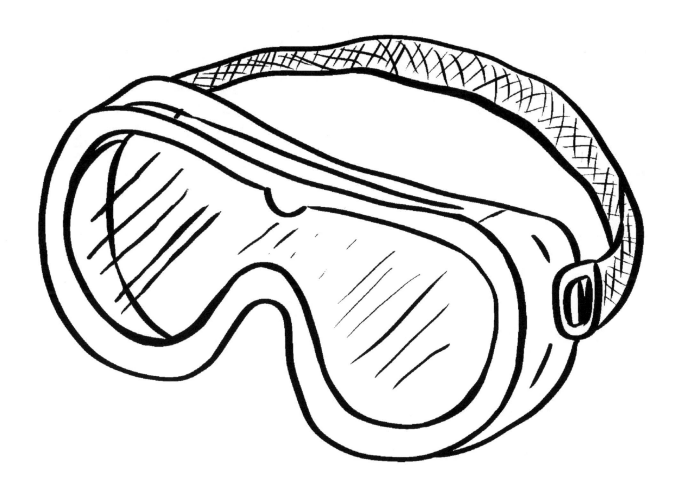

Goggles

Minnow

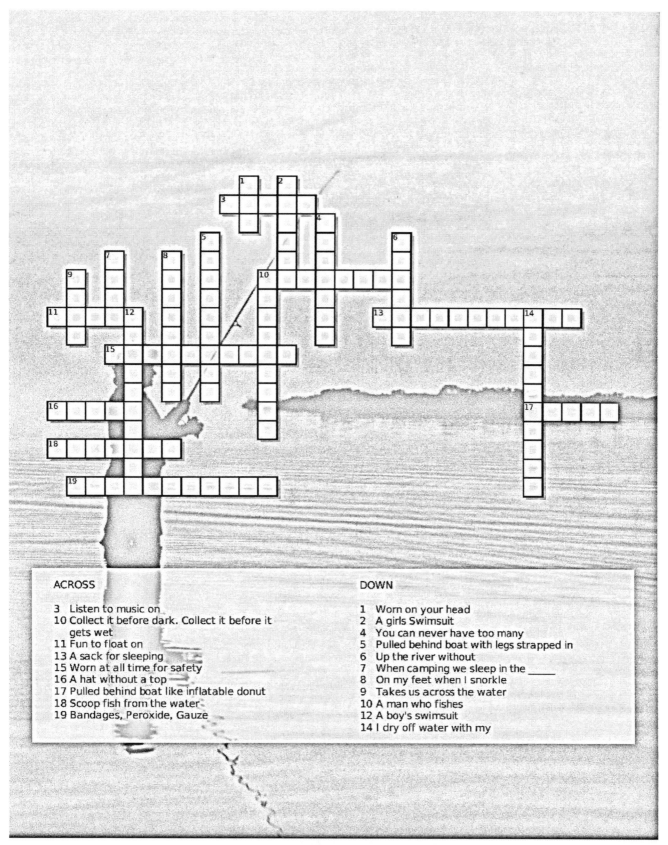

ACROSS

3 Listen to music on
10 Collect it before dark. Collect it before it gets wet
11 Fun to float on
13 A sack for sleeping
15 Worn at all time for safety
16 A hat without a top
17 Pulled behind boat like inflatable donut
18 Scoop fish from the water
19 Bandages, Peroxide, Gauze

DOWN

1 Worn on your head
2 A girls Swimsuit
4 You can never have too many
5 Pulled behind boat with legs strapped in
6 Up the river without
7 When camping we sleep in the _____
8 On my feet when I snorkle
9 Takes us across the water
10 A man who fishes
12 A boy's swimsuit
14 I dry off water with my

Solve the Puzzle

Marshmallows

Light House

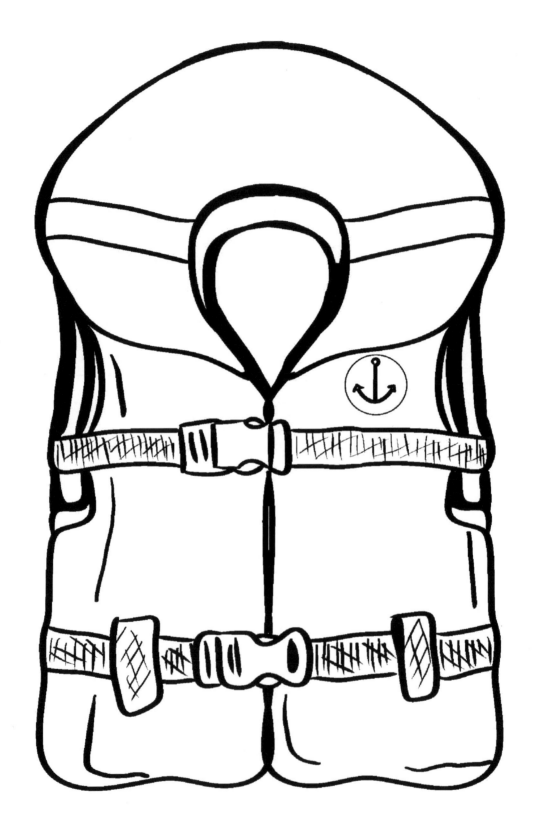

Life Jacket

Paddle Boat

Playing Cards

A	I	T	O	C	C	R	I	C	K	E	T	D	I
E	X	C	A	U	H	L	Q	F	A	V	B	Z	L
K	L	I	A	C	B	A	P	I	R	O	C	K	S
T	I	T	S	M	K	A	I	R	O	D	G	J	B
U	L	P	J	G	E	L	A	R	F	H	C	D	R
A	N	C	H	O	R	R	E	K	S	I	Y	R	K
C	S	N	A	C	K	S	A	C	A	R	D	S	V
D	O	C	B	O	T	T	L	E	I	P	O	F	C
E	B	O	O	C	S	P	F	J	B	O	O	K	L
Q	W	D	Z	O	Q	L	J	W	S	U	K	M	O
V	O	Z	G	I	L	C	J	F	J	H	E	Z	T
U	R	R	I	X	E	E	X	Y	T	N	O	P	H
G	M	O	H	N	L	A	R	X	M	Z	B	E	E
Z	S	Z	B	I	N	O	C	U	L	A	R	C	S

How Many Lake Fun Words Can You Find?

Picnic Basket

Cellular Phone

Snacks

S'more

Small Mouth Bass

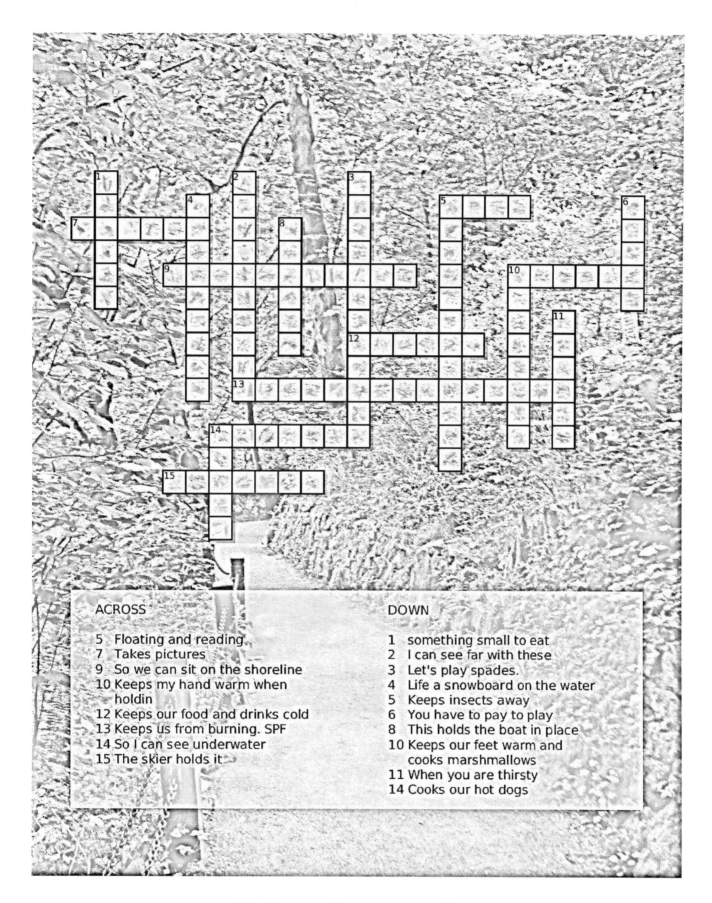

ACROSS

5 Floating and reading
7 Takes pictures
9 So we can sit on the shoreline
10 Keeps my hand warm when holdin
12 Keeps our food and drinks cold
13 Keeps us from burning. SPF
14 So I can see underwater
15 The skier holds it

DOWN

1 something small to eat
2 I can see far with these
3 Let's play spades.
4 Life a snowboard on the water
5 Keeps insects away
6 You have to pay to play
8 This holds the boat in place
10 Keeps our feet warm and cooks marshmallows
11 When you are thirsty
14 Cooks our hot dogs

Solve the Puzzle!

Sleeping Bag

Trash

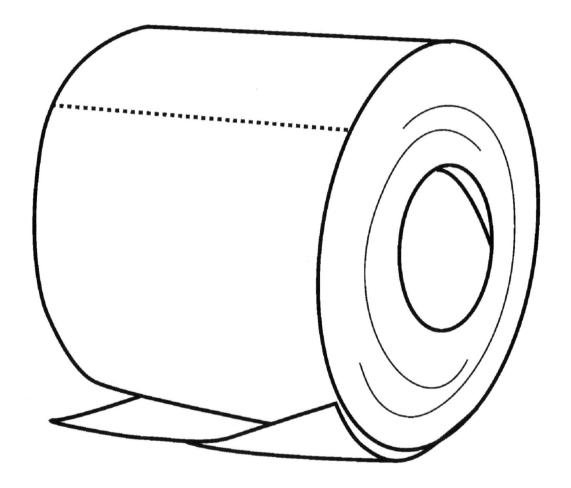

Toilet Paper

Tent

Tackle Box

Circle Items You Could Wear to the Lake.

Worms

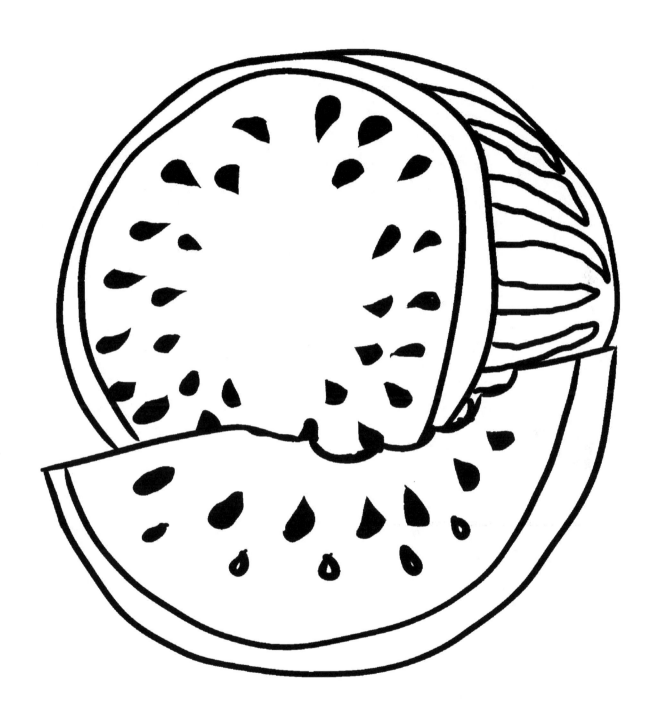

Water Melon

Snake

Water Shoes

Water Bottle

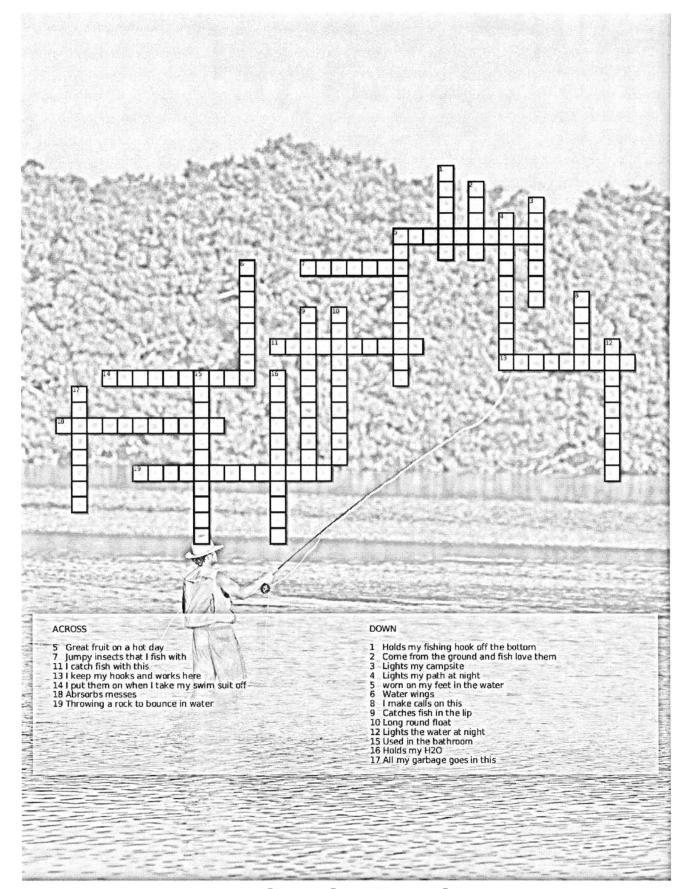

ACROSS

5 Great fruit on a hot day
7 Jumpy insects that I fish with
11 I catch fish with this
13 I keep my hooks and works here
14 I put them on when I take my swim suit off
18 Abrsorbs messes
19 Throwing a rock to bounce in water

DOWN

1 Holds my fishing hook off the bottom
2 Come from the ground and fish love them
3 Lights my campsite
4 Lights my path at night
5 worn on my feet in the water
6 Water wings
8 I make calls on this
9 Catches fish in the lip
10 Long round float
12 Lights the water at night
15 Used in the bathroom
16 Holds my H2O
17 All my garbage goes in this

Solve the Puzzle

Wake Board

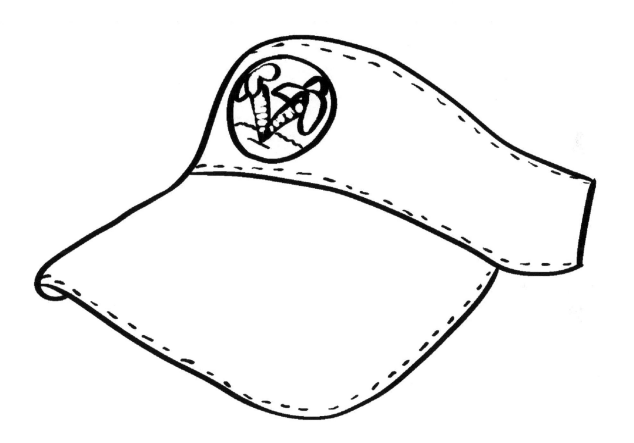

Visor

Turtle

Tubes

Trout

Swim Trunks

Tablet

Swim Noodle

Swim Cap

Sun Screen

Skipping Rocks

Ski Rope

Seagull

Q	B	P	V	D	P	R	S	D	U	C	K	P	W
M	I	N	N	O	W	W	P	H	O	N	E	A	A
E	T	J	K	G	T	U	R	T	L	E	K	P	T
F	G	R	G	C	A	T	F	I	S	H	T	E	E
I	I	E	O	I	Q	C	B	D	A	Z	R	R	R
S	B	O	A	T	R	R	L	O	F	O	A	V	M
H	Q	P	W	H	T	I	U	A	B	X	S	X	E
I	P	V	A	K	S	C	E	K	X	D	H	U	L
N	W	H	T	D	K	K	G	R	E	B	E	U	O
G	N	H	E	K	I	E	I	L	U	E	Y	C	N
M	I	I	R	C	U	T	L	C	N	J	F	U	I
T	I	D	Y	T	A	G	L	C	J	L	O	J	U
L	U	U	L	Q	B	O	B	B	E	R	P	C	T
Q	T	X	L	A	N	T	E	R	N	C	O	A	A

How Many Lake Fun Words Can You Find?

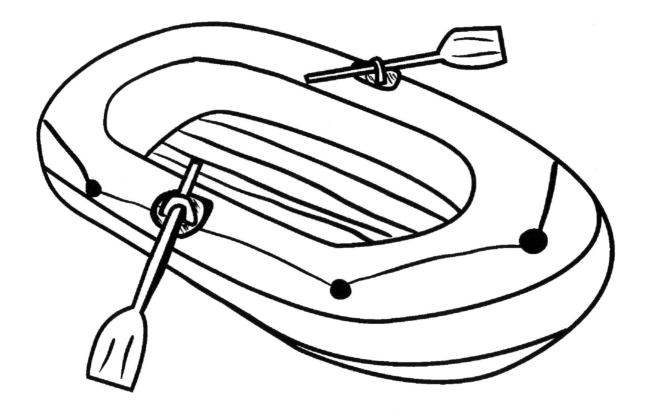

Raft

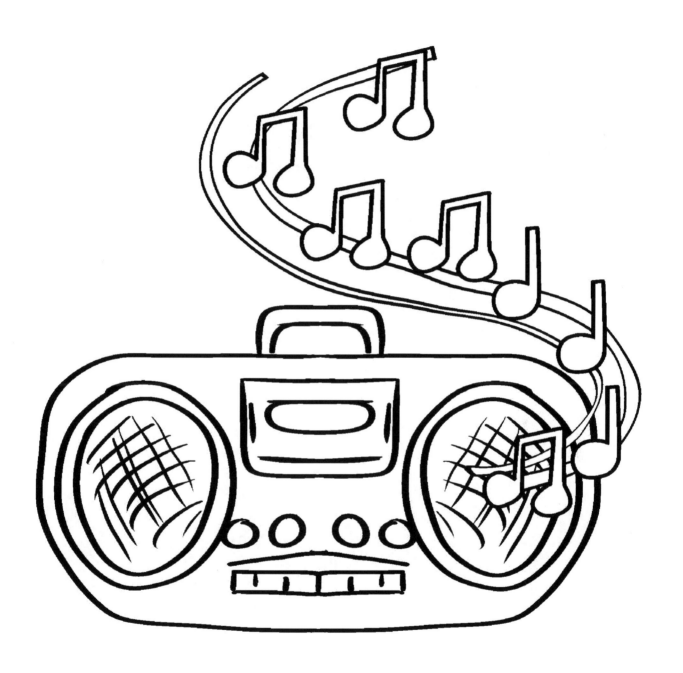

Radio

Popsicle

Pelican

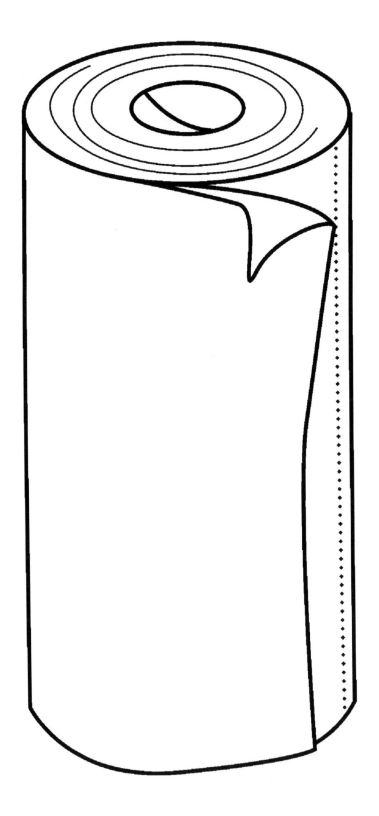

Paper Towel

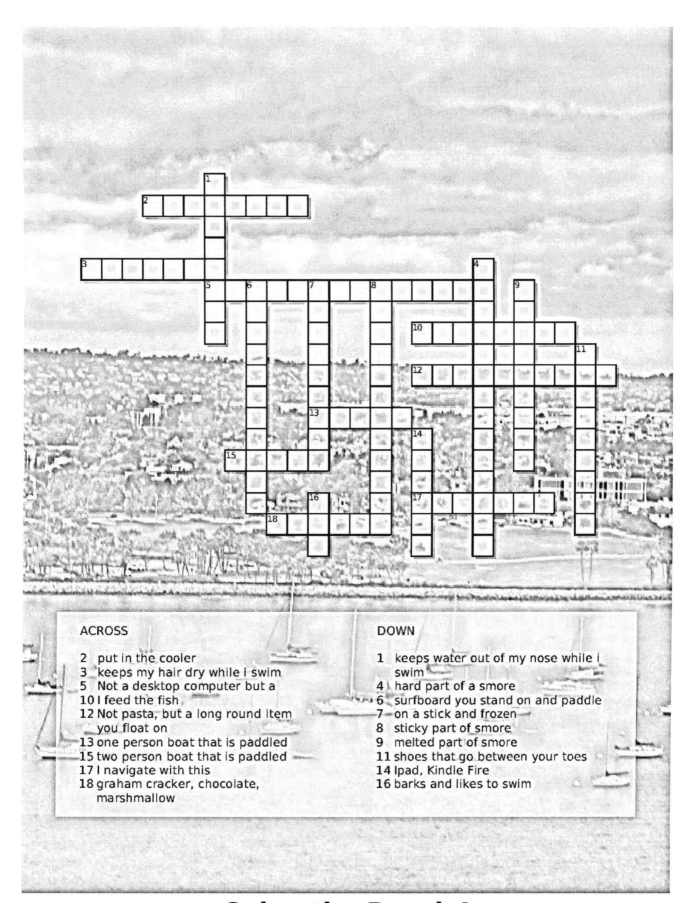

ACROSS

2 put in the cooler
3 keeps my hair dry while i swim
5 Not a desktop computer but a
10 I feed the fish
12 Not pasta, but a long round item
   you float on
13 one person boat that is paddled
15 two person boat that is paddled
17 I navigate with this
18 graham cracker, chocolate,
   marshmallow

DOWN

1 keeps water out of my nose while i
   swim
4 hard part of a smore
6 surfboard you stand on and paddle
7 on a stick and frozen
8 sticky part of smore
9 melted part of smore
11 shoes that go between your toes
14 Ipad, Kindle Fire
16 barks and likes to swim

Solve the Puzzle!

Paddle Board

Canoe

Nose Plug

Money

www.LakeFun.com

Large Mouth Bass

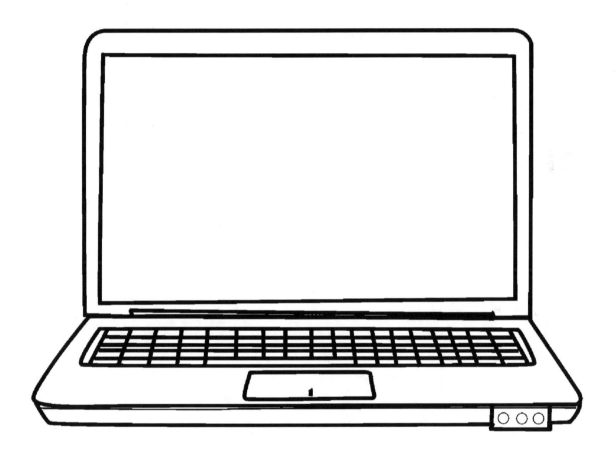

Laptop

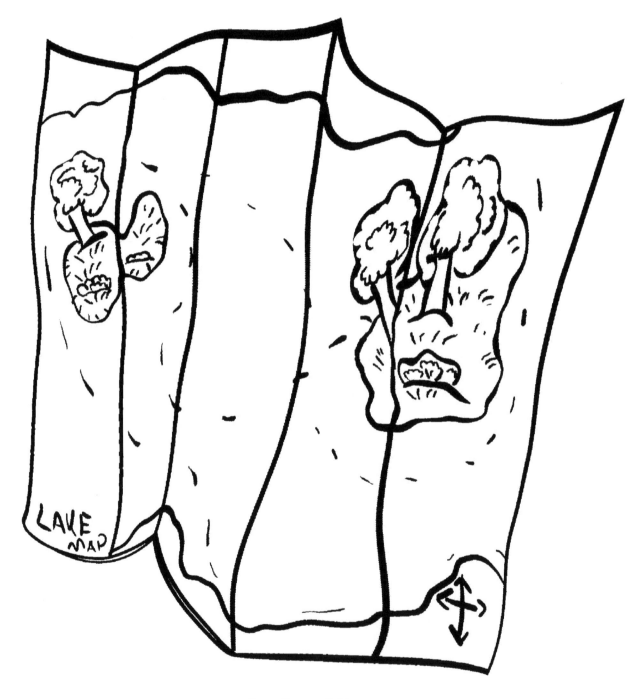

Lake Map

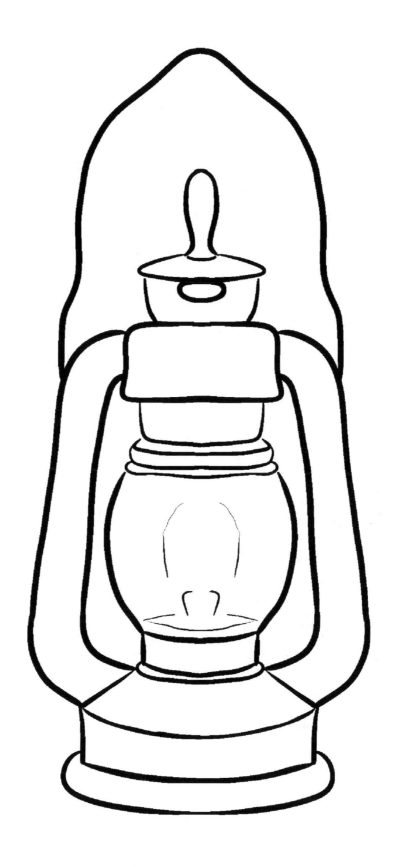

Lantern

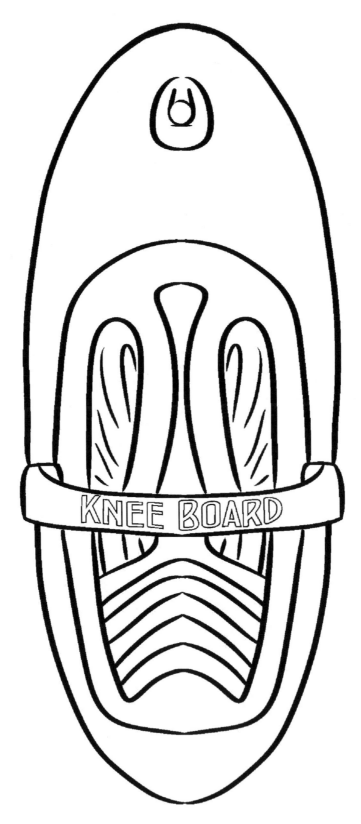

Knee Board

Dock

Frog

Friends

G	P	E	L	I	C	A	N	F	F	Q	G	S
T	A	B	L	E	T	K	R	I	C	E	F	M
A	L	L	H	P	L	U	G	O	L	S	X	O
S	R	E	S	L	H	F	F	B	A	S	S	R
E	X	C	A	L	W	A	O	X	X	S	A	E
M	Z	A	N	A	H	D	O	T	Y	E	X	S
P	Q	N	D	P	B	H	D	R	B	A	V	G
O	V	O	A	T	A	D	D	O	N	G	V	G
K	Z	E	L	O	G	Y	O	U	F	U	F	F
D	L	F	S	P	D	A	G	T	A	L	R	U
H	C	H	O	C	O	L	A	T	E	L	O	N
K	A	Y	A	K	U	G	L	A	K	E	G	N
T	S	W	I	M	F	O	L	D	D	Q	N	C

How Many Lake Fun Words Can You Find?

Floaties

Lake Chair

Blue Gill

Boat Light

Camera

Campfire

Lake Shore

Catfish

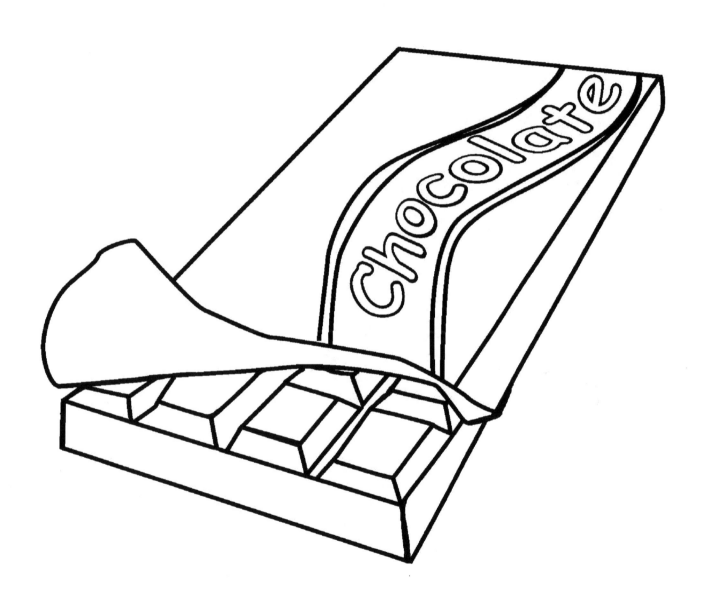

Chocolate

Cooler

Lake Clothes

Duck

Firewood

First Aid Kit

Fish Food

Fish Net

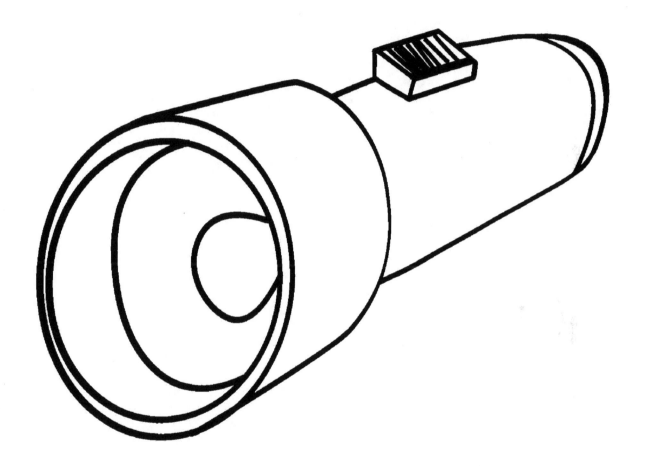

Flash Light

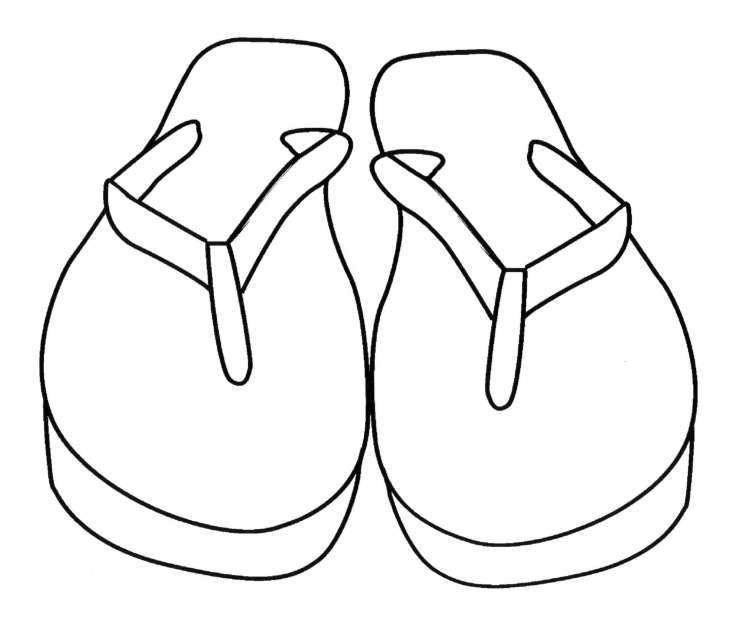

Flip Flops

Flippers

(Sample ½ page advertisement only $149 per year)

Advertise with us!

Do you own a family oriented business or organization that makes your lake more fun?

Advertise in this **Lake Fun Book** for a low introductory cost of $149 for a half page or $199 for a full page for a full year.

Plus a FREE basic listing on www.LakeFun.com

For more information e-mail: Jobe@LakeFun.com TODAY!

About the Author

Jobe Leonard lives in Dandridge, TN. After attending Tennessee Technological University, he received his MBA at Lincoln Memorial University. He has over 20 titles published on travel, construction, and architecture. He is a project manager with Hearthstone Homes and has currently built over 150 custom log and timber homes in 30 different states. This includes a recent project he managed that was named the 2012 National Log Home of the Year. For more information on his current projects, visit www.Jobe.ws.

If you enjoyed reading this guide I would appreciate your honest review on Amazon, Facebook, or Twitter. Also tell a friend and help me spread the word. Send any questions to JobeLeonard@gmail.com

Made in the USA
Columbia, SC
05 June 2025

59000049R00059